YOU MIGHT BE FROM ALBERTA IF...

Dave Elston

MacIntyre Purcell Publishing Inc.
194 Hospital Rd.
Lunenburg, Nova Scotia
B0J 2C0
(902) 640-3350

www.macintyrepurcell.com
info@macintyrepurcell.com

Printed and bound in Canada by Marquis.

Library and Archives Canada Cataloguing in Publication

Elston, Dave, 1958-, author   You might be from Alberta if... / David Elston.

ISBN 978-1-927097-87-8 (pbk.)

     1. Alberta--Social life and customs--Caricatures and cartoons.   2. Canadian wit and humor, Pictorial.   3. Comic books, strips, etc.   I. Title.

FC3661.3.E47 2015   971.23   C2015-903115-X

MacIntyre Purcell Publishing Inc. would like to acknowledge the financial support of the Government of Canada through Department of Canadian Heritage (Canada Book Fund) and the Nova Scotia Department of Tourism, Culture and Heritage.

FOREWORD

I am a proud Albertan. I was born in Alberta. Heck, my grandmother's name was Alberta, God rest her soul.

I still remember visiting my great-grandfather in The Crowsnest Pass, Coleman area. I think about him when I see Dave's drawings, because Grandpa Phillips had a squinty half-closed eye, a permanent grin, and a wrinkled face of leather, tanned by the sun and etched by years of chain smoking, mountain wind, and the hard life that comes with mining coal. Most of The Pass has that kind of twisted beauty, part self-inflicted, but mostly born of the blood, sweat, and tears of a pioneering work ethic, drawing a life from the sometimes tight-gripped resources of our bountiful, fragile landscape.

Grandpa Phillips loved watching The Chucks and Stampede Wrestling. He had strong opinions, which he mostly kept to himself. He was a real-life Dave character; as if he'd jumped off one of Dave's pages, or out of Dave's mind.

Alberta, while it has clear stereotypes and iconic subject matter, is a subtle and complex place. It welcomes all with a slight wariness, insisting a newcomer prove his or her trustworthiness, often by done by showing up to help a neighbour, instead of offering.

I've seen a lot of changes in Alberta in my lifetime. Modernization, population growth, and shifting politics all rise and fall with popular opinion and an uptick in the price of oil. Through it all, Alberta remains as constant as my grandmother's "coal miner's daughter" afternoon coffee, cigarette, and bread baking.

Alberta has a soul, and it's made of black soil, chinook winds, independence, and neighbourly love. She wears a Bible belt, and seeks to offer opportunity and blessing to anyone who will love her with a pure heart, and a sacrificial spirit.

Dave's done something really special in "*You Might Be From Alberta If...*" to capture all of these things. Dave Elston's whimsical art and wry wit combine to capture the ethos of Alberta.

— Paul Brandt

INTRODUCTION

Near as I can tell, one fine September day, John MacIntyre, the publisher of this book, was dialing random phone numbers and asking whoever answered on the other end if they'd like to do a book on the quirks and idiosyncrasies of being an Albertan.

Luckily for me, I was one of those phone numbers. Normally cartoonists are very wary of publishers, but it's hard to ignore one whose only demands are "have some fun with it and we'll talk when you're done."

It wouldn't have been nearly as much fun without the contributions of fellow Albertans Graeme Morton and Jack Tennant. (I'm sooooo glad they only write and don't draw!)

Other Albertans contributed inadvertently, in that they had an interesting observation or story, and I shamelessly turned it into a cartoon. Betty Park, Gene Danysk, Brent Lemay, Lorne Wooden, Debbie, Danielle, and Jeffrey Lee would fall into that category.

So take a little tour through these pages. *You Might Be From Alberta If . . .* you spot you or your friends in some of these cartoons.

— *Dave Elston*

YOU MIGHT BE FROM ALBERTA IF...

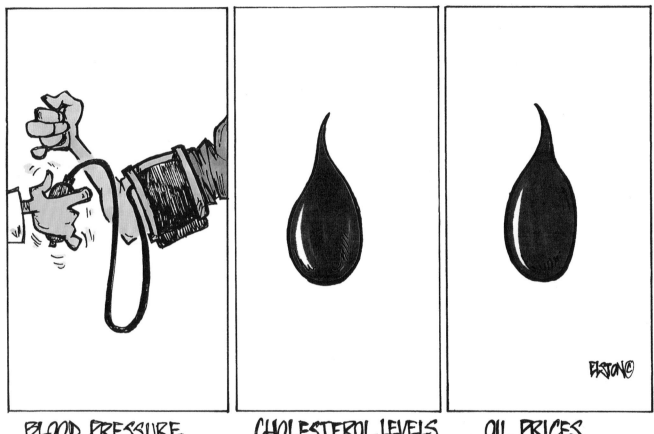

YOU THINK THE THREE NUMBERS CRUCIAL TO GOOD HEALTH ARE...

BLOOD PRESSURE   CHOLESTEROL LEVELS   OIL PRICES

YOU'VE DRIVEN THE ENTIRE QEZ IN THE LEFT LANE

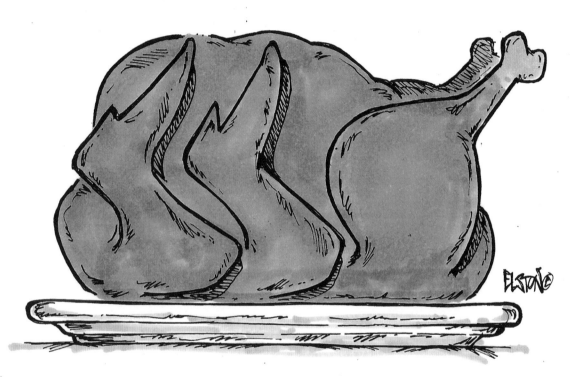

YOUR THANKSGIVING TURKEY HAD TWO RIGHT WINGS

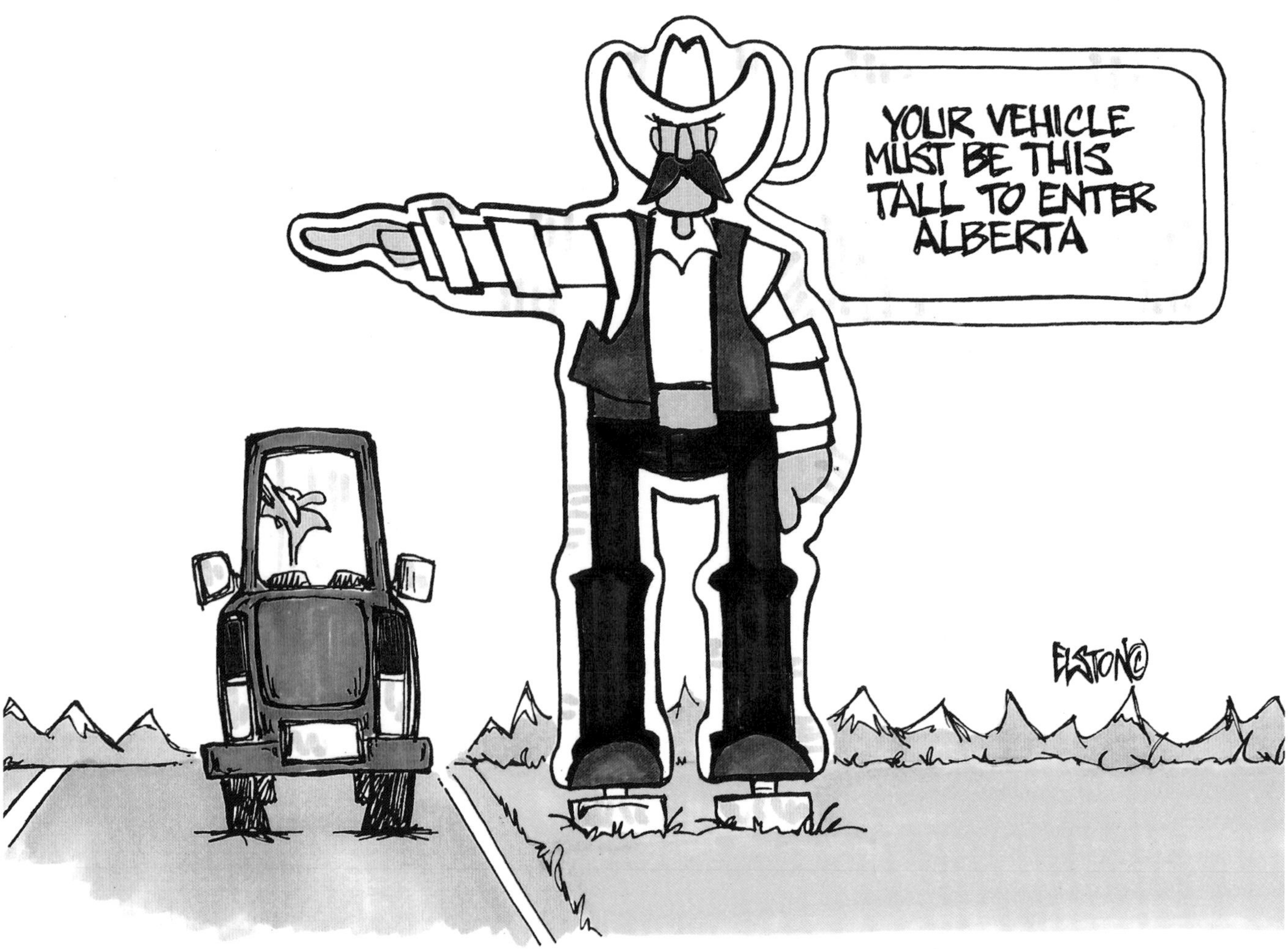
YOUR VEHICLE MUST BE THIS TALL TO ENTER ALBERTA
ELSTON©

YOU'RE CONVINCED ALL ROADS ENTERING ALBERTA HAVE THESE SIGNS

YOU LEARNED THE THREE R's **AND** THE THREE S's.

YOU THINK "BI-CURIOUS" MEANS THAT YOU'RE THINKING ABOUT TAKING FRENCH LESSONS.

YOUR FRIEND FROM ONTARIO SENDS YOU
BOXERS FOR YOUR TRUCK NUTS.

SNIFF
SNIFF
SNIFF

INSTEAD OF PERFUME OR COLOGNE, YOUR FAVOURITE MAGAZINE HAS BEAR SPRAY SAMPLES.

YOU THINK DRIVE-THRU WINDOWS ARE TOO LOW

BOTH YOUR JEANS AND YOUR WINDSHIELD ARE STONE-WASHED

YOU'RE THE ONE **NOT** WEARING GREEN AT A STAMPS GAME

THE FRONT DOORS TO YOUR HOUSE ARE SALOON DOORS.

YOU RAISE URBAN CHICKENS.

YOU KNOW THAT SAG-D IS NOT SOMETHING THAT HAPPENS TO WOMEN'S BREASTS

YOUR LEXUS HAS FARM LICENCE PLATES.

YOU'VE SEEN THE ICE FOR THE CFL WEST FINAL BE BETTER THAN THE ICE FOR THE NHL OUTDOOR GAME.

YOU HAVE A DECISION TO MAKE WHEN YOUR FLIGHT IS FORCED TO MAKE AN EMERGENCY LANDING AT TRUDEAU AIRPORT.

WHILE DRIVING UNDER A PLUS-15 YOU DISCOVER THAT YOUR LOAD IS PLUS-16.

YOUR BIKE RIDE IS INTERRUPTED BY A CATTLE DRIVE, SUDDENLY MAKING YOU WISH YOUR BIKE HAD FENDERS.

YOU STILL GIGGLE WHEN YOU TALK ABOUT STIMULATING A WELL.

YOU'RE FAMILIAR WITH THE CLASSIC CHILDREN'S FAIRY TALE "LITTLE RED RIDING NECK."

YOU'VE EXPERIENCED A CHINOOK HEADACHE

YOU'LL ONLY GO HIKING WITH SOMEONE SLOWER THAN YOU.

SWITCHING FROM BARBED WIRE TO PLANK FENCING IS YOUR IDEA OF GOING WIRELESS.

YOU KNOW THE THREE MAIN TYPES OF DANCING ARE...

SQUARE

UKRAINIAN

AROUND-THE-ISSUES

YOU CALL THEM BEAR BELLS, THEY CALL THEM DINNER BELLS.

YOU CAN'T UNDERSTAND WHY PRO WRESTLING CHAMPIONSHIP BELT BUCKLES ARE SO SMALL

THE OIL COMPANY YOU WORK FOR DOESN'T USE CLAY PIGEONS AT THEIR SKEET-SHOOTING EVENT ANYMORE.

"WHERE THE DEER AND THE ANTELOPE PLAY" IS USUALLY RIGHT IN FRONT OF YOUR CAR.

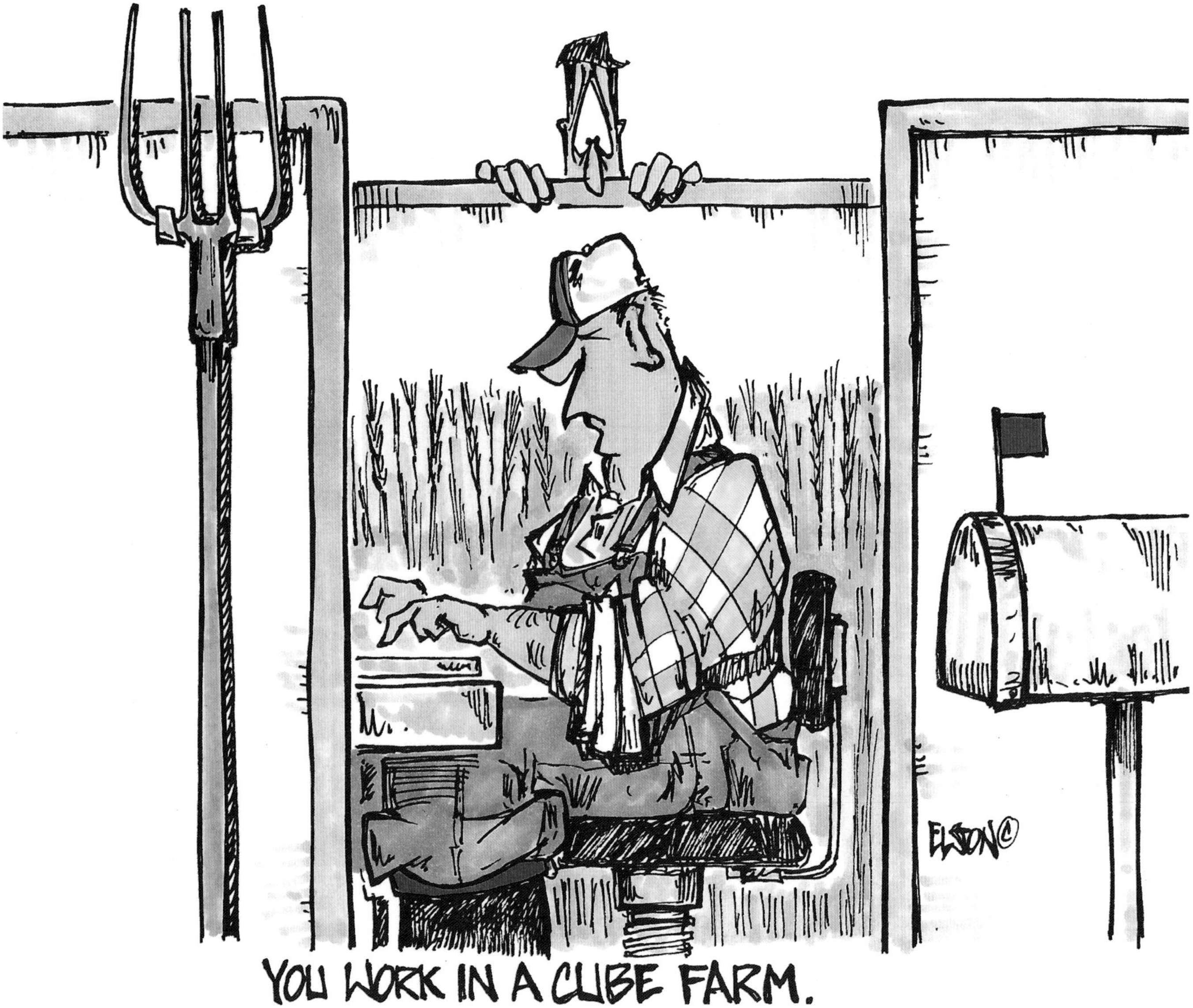
ELSON©

YOU WORK IN A CUBE FARM.

YOU KNOW THERE'S THREE TYPES OF BABY BOOTIES.

YOU THINK PAUL BRANDT'S "ALBERTA BOUND" SHOULD BE THE PROVINCIAL ANTHEM.

YOU'RE PRETTY SURE IAN TYSON COULD WHUP MIKE TYSON

YOU ONLY PAID $500,000.⁰⁰ FOR YOUR HOUSE IN FT. McMURRAY.

YOU KNOW THAT "FOUR STRONG WINDS" AREN'T THE ONLY THINGS THAT BLOW.

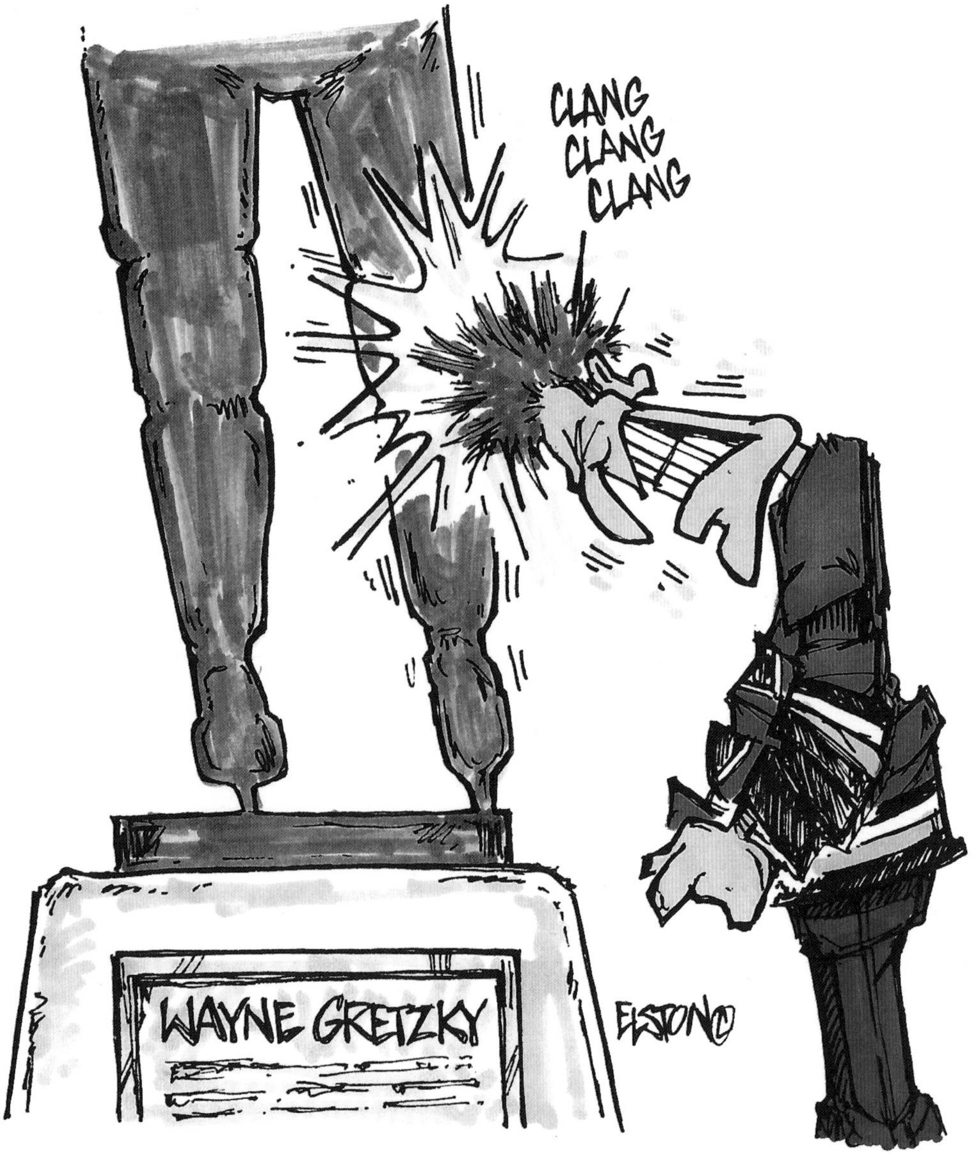
CLANG
CLANG
CLANG
WAYNE GRETZKY
ELSTON©

YOU LOVE THE GRETZKY STATUE...
UNLESS YOU'RE FROM CALGARY.

YOU LOVE THE TOUCHDOWN HORSE... UNLESS YOU'RE FROM EDMONTON.

YOU START YOUR DIESEL TRUCK IN NOVEMBER
AND LEAVE IT RUNNING UNTIL MARCH

FOR MOVEMBER YOU GROW A MOUSTACHE. AND SO DOES YOUR HUSBAND.

THE GREEN ONE, THE BLACK ONE, AND THE BLUE ONE IS YOUR BUCKET LIST.

WAIT TIMES ARE SO BAD THE GUY IN LINE BEHIND YOU IS AN E.R. DOCTOR.

YOUR TODDLER GETS HER FIRST SET OF BUILDING BLOCKS AND SPELLS...

YOU'VE SHOPPED IN EVERY SINGLE STORE IN WEST EDMONTON MALL.

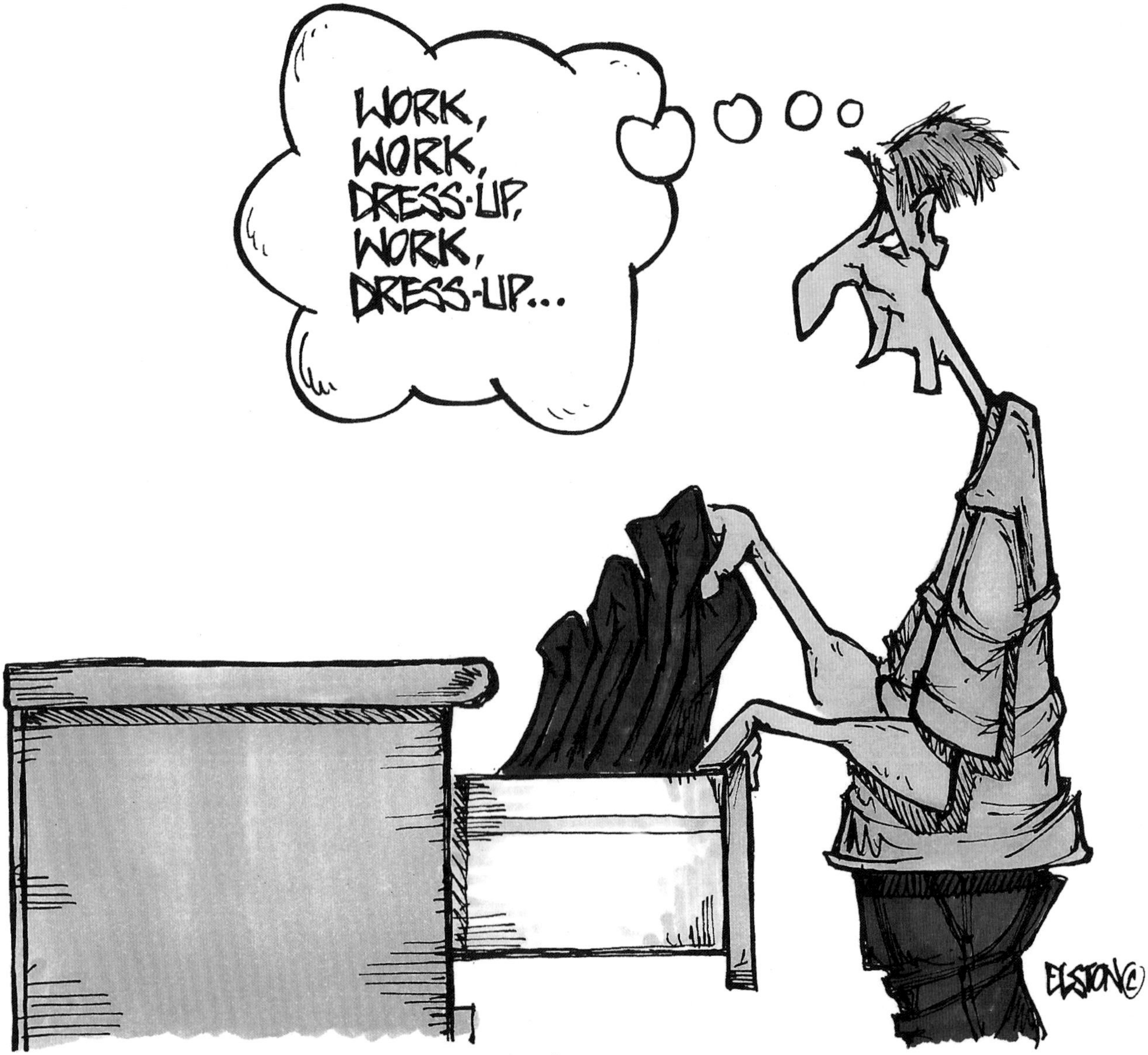
WORK,
WORK,
DRESS-UP,
WORK,
DRESS-UP...
ELSTON©

YOUR JEAN POOL CONSISTS OF...

SOMETIMES YOU HAVE THE WORLD'S COOLEST NIGHT LIGHT.

YOU CAN THINK INSIDE **AND** OUTSIDE THE BOX.

YOU BOUGHT YOUR "BEETS" IN TABER.

ONE OF YOUR SCHOOL'S PHYS-ED OPTIONS IS MUTTON-BUSTIN'

CLIMBING THROUGH A BARBED-WIRE FENCE ALWAYS YIELDS THE SAME RESULTS.

YOU LIKE THE IDEA OF CORPORATE BRANDING

YOUR GOLF COURSE HAS AN OILSAND-TRAP.

YOUR CAMO GEAR BLOWS OFF THE CLOTHESLINE AND YOU CAN'T FIND IT.

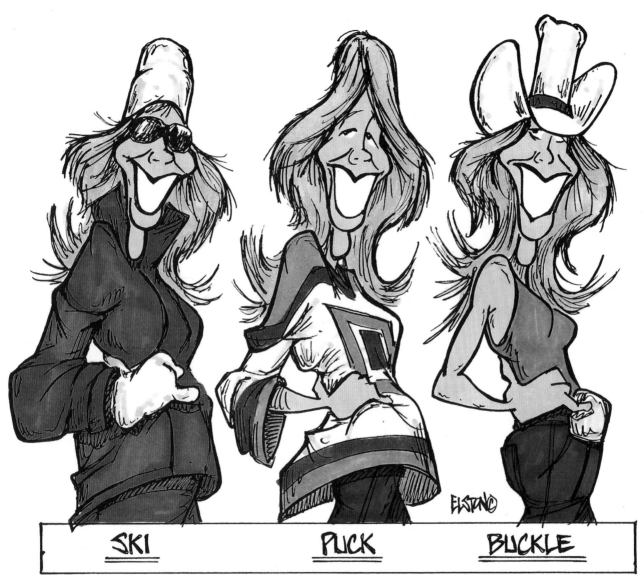

SKI   PUCK   BUCKLE

YOU KNOW THE THREE MAIN SPECIES OF BUNNIES.

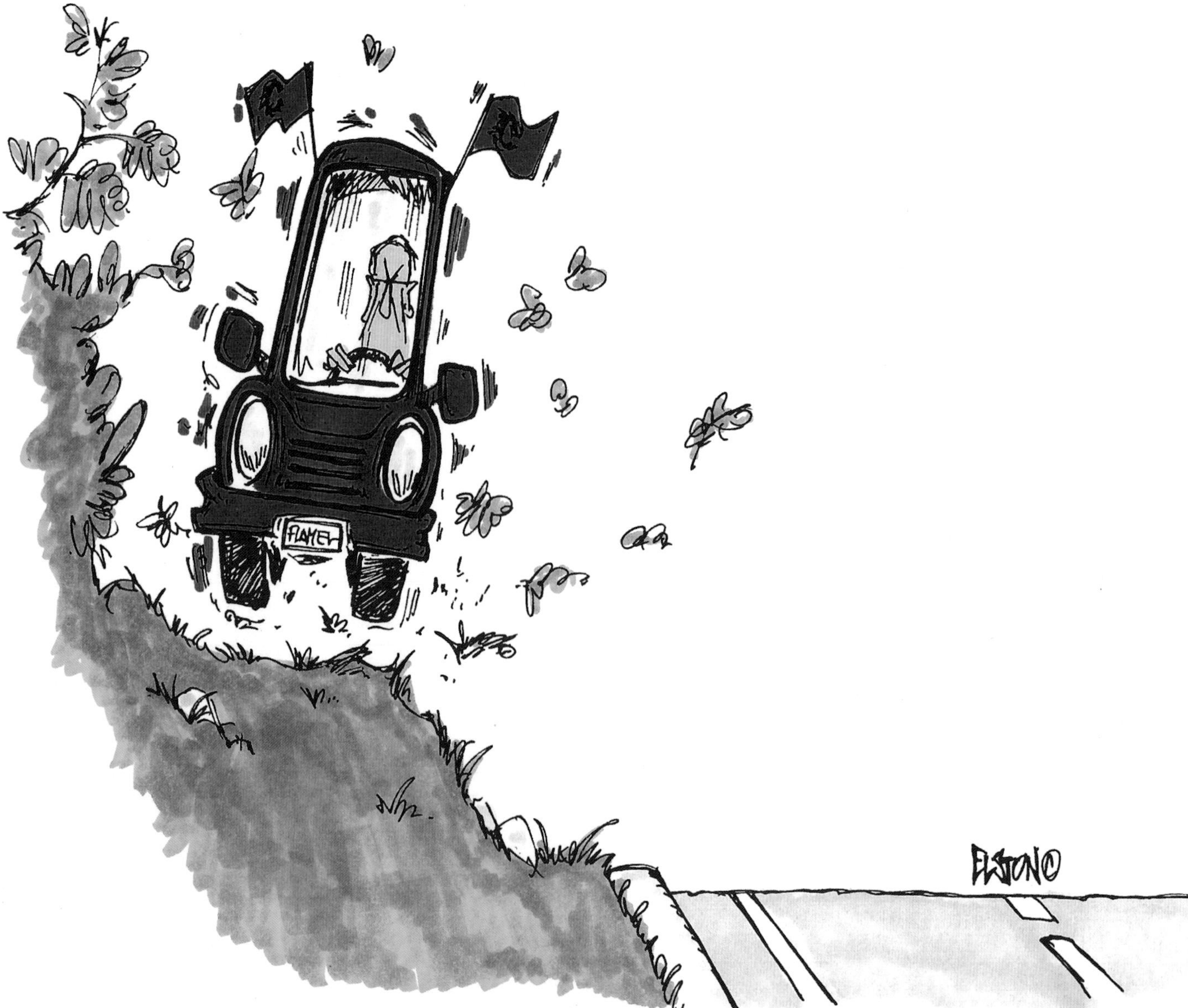
ELSTON©

YOU'RE A FLAMES FAN AND THERE'S NO WAY YOU'RE TRAVELLING ON "WAYNE GRETZKY DRIVE."

YOU CONSIDER EVERYTHING EAST OF MEDICINE HAT, DOWN EAST.

YOU'VE BEEN DRIVING FOR YEARS AND YOU **STILL** WONDER WHAT THAT LEVER ON THE LEFT IS FOR.

YOU STARTED A TAILINGS POND HOCKEY LEAGUE.

YOU ENJOY SHOE SHOPPING

THIS IS YOUR IDEA OF A CAT TREE.

YOU LEARNED ALL YOUR WRESTLING TERMINOLOGY FROM ED WHALEN.

YOU REMEMBER WHEN IT WASN'T RAT-FREE.

YOUR IDEA OF CLASSICAL MUSIC IS
BUCKSHOT AND BENNY'S, "16 CHICKENS AND A TAMBOURINE."

YOU HAVE A FRIEND IN BC WHO'S PRETTY SURE THE MAD COW CRISIS COULD HAVE BEEN AVOIDED WITH ANGER MANAGEMENT THERAPY.

YOU THINK THIS IS THE OFFICIAL FLAG OF FT. MCMURRAY

YOU OWN A REUSABLE BUMPER STICKER.

YOU BET YOUR FRIEND FROM TORONTO THAT
HE CAN'T PEE OVER AN ELECTRIC FENCE.

YOU'VE MISUNDERSTOOD THE "BRING YOUR KID TO WORK" MEMO.

YOU DRIVE INSTEAD OF FLY FROM CALGARY TO EDMONTON "CUZ IT'S FASTER."

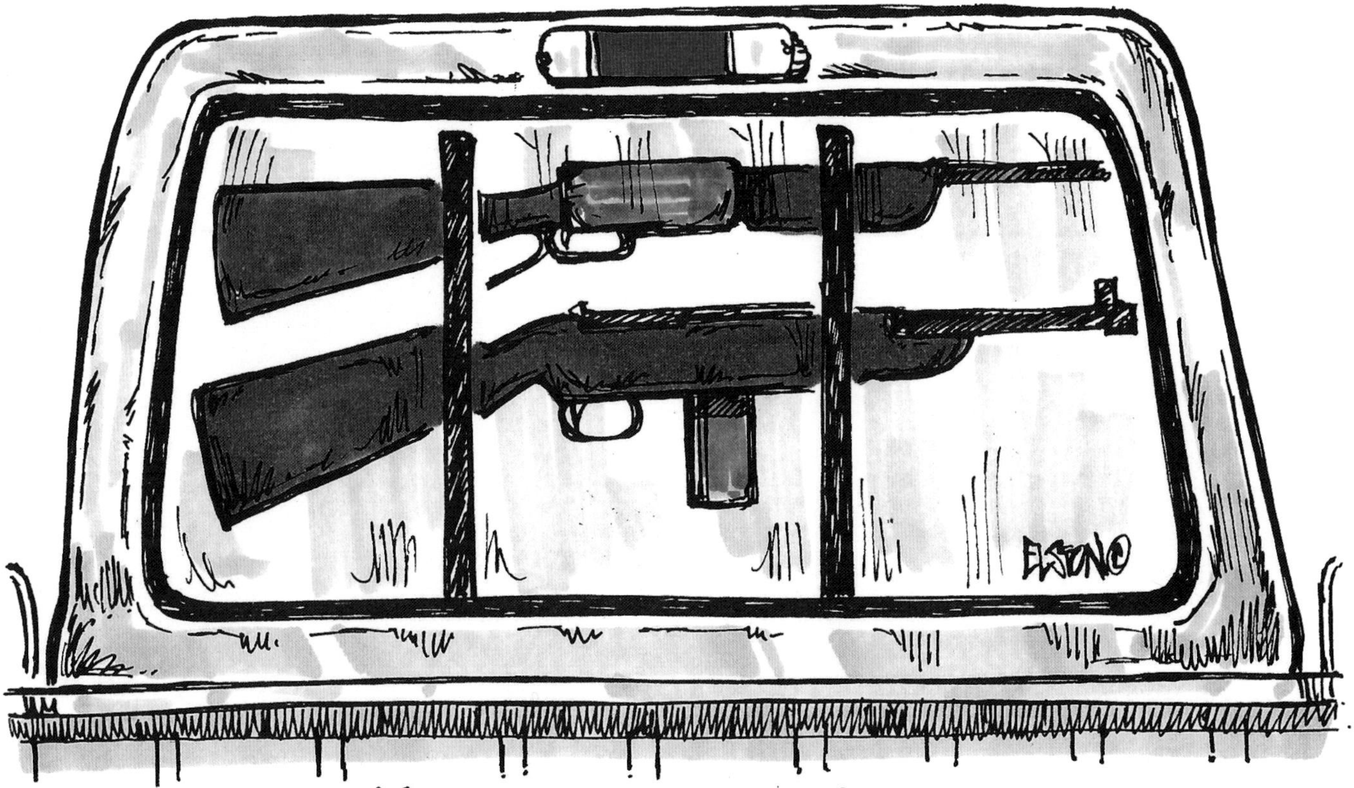
ELSON©

YOU HAVE A NICE RACK.

YOUR WHITE COLLAR IS ACTUALLY A NECK TATTOO.

YOUR LAWN ORNAMENTS EAT WHILE YOU SLEEP.

YOU KNOW THAT THEY MAY NOT GROW GRAPES BUT THE FARMERS CAN STILL MAKE A FINE WHINE.

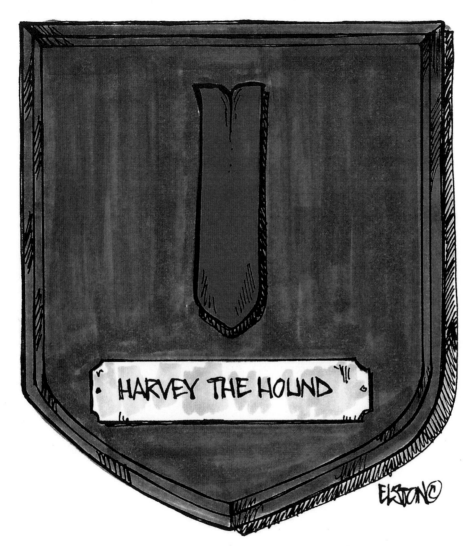

YOU'VE SEEN CRAIG MACTAVISH'S TROPHY ROOM

YOU SPENT MORE ON YOUR TRUCK THAN YOUR EDUCATION.

YOU'VE VISITED ONE OF ITS GHOST TOWNS.

BOTH YOUR SON **AND** YOUR CATTLE HAVE PIERCED EARS.

YOU CAN HOLD A SHOTGUN SHELL TO YOUR EAR AND HEAR THE OCEAN.

YOU ONLY HAVE TWO BALE CONDITIONS — ROUND AND SQUARE.

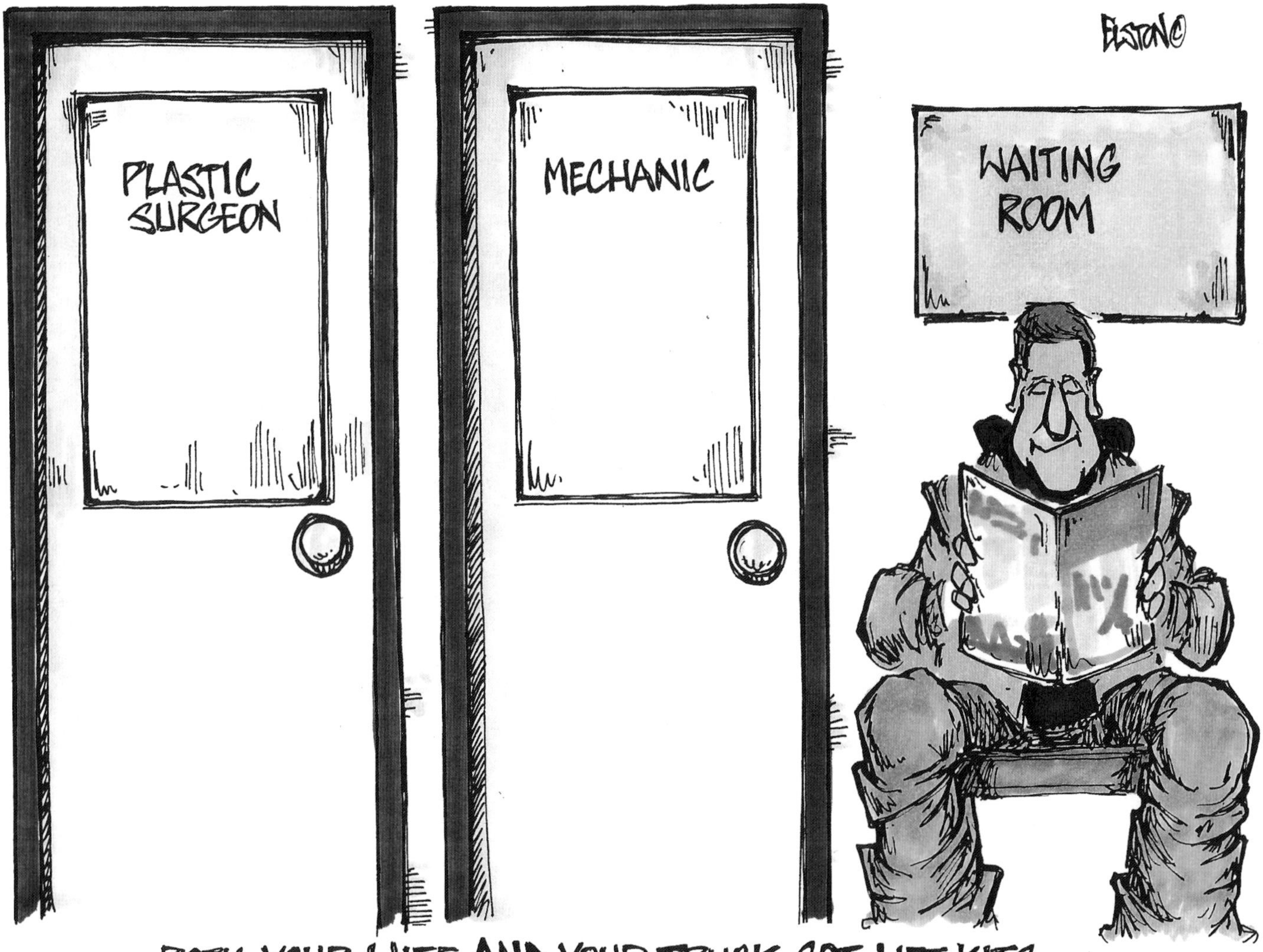
ELSTON©
PLASTIC SURGEON
MECHANIC
WAITING ROOM

BOTH YOUR WIFE AND YOUR TRUCK GOT LIFT KITS.

YOU'VE SUFFERED FROSTBITE WHILE BARBECUING.

YOUR KID READS LOCALLY WRITTEN BEDTIME STORIES

DEEP DOWN YOU'D LOVE TO SEE THE SUTTER BROTHERS PLAY THE HANSON BROTHERS.

YOU KNOW THAT ANGELS DON'T HAVE WINGS, THEY HAVE ROTORS.

YOUR ROCK COLLECTION HAS HANDLES.

"DEBIT OR CREDIT?" MEANS YOU'RE TRYING TO DECIDE WHICH CARD TO SCRAPE YOUR WINDSHIELD WITH.

YOUR REMOTE CAR STARTER AND AUTOMATIC GARAGE DOOR OPENER ALSO SHOVELS YOUR DRIVEWAY.

YOU JUMP-START PEOPLE'S VEHICLES WITH YOUR PACEMAKER.

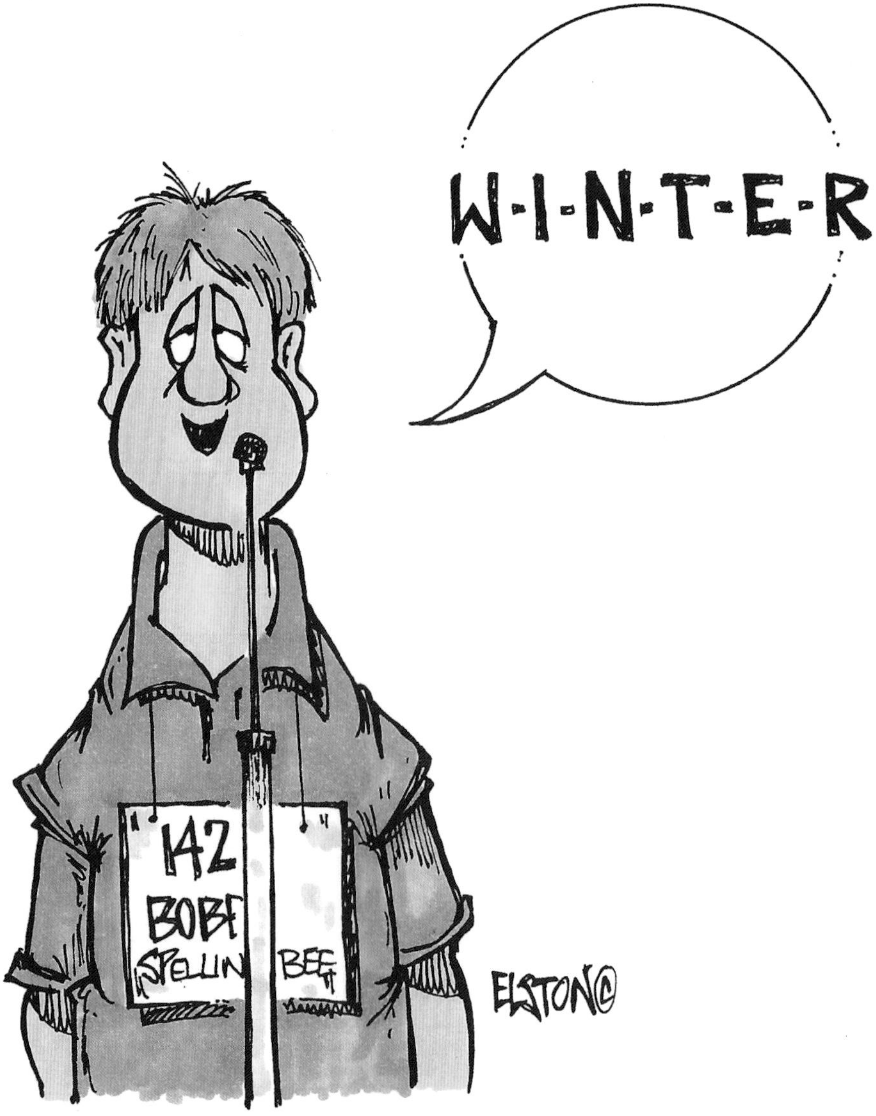
W-I-N-T-E-R
142
ELSTON©

YOU SPELL POLAR VORTEX...

A GUY APPROACHING YOUR BANK TILL WHILE WEARING A BALACLAVA DOESN'T NECESSARILY MEAN YOU'RE BEING ROBBED.

YOU'RE TOBOGGANING ... AND A CHINOOK HITS.

HALFWAY THROUGH GETTING YOUR CAR WASHED, THE CHINOOK ENDS.

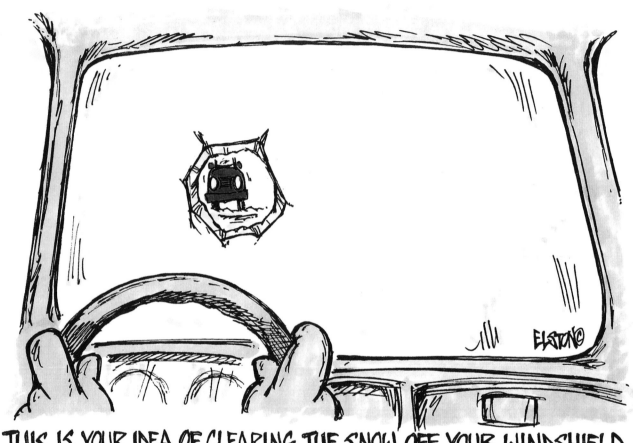

THIS IS YOUR IDEA OF CLEARING THE SNOW OFF YOUR WINDSHIELD

"PIMPING YOUR RIDE" MEANS PUTTING CARDBOARD OVER YOUR RADIATOR.

YOU SPEND JANUARY IN ONE OF THESE NEIGHBOURHOODS

| RIVERDALE | MARTINDALE | SCOTTSDALE |

YOU'RE THE ONE WEARING STEEL-TOED FLIP-FLOPS

YOU'VE HEARD THAT TAKING VITAMIN D HELPS MAKE UP FOR THE LACK OF SUNLIGHT IN WINTER

YOU'RE GOING WHEREVER THE SNOWPLOW IS.

SOMEWHERE BETWEEN HIGH LEVEL AND INDIAN CABINS YOUR GPS JUST SHRUGS.

YOUR ANTI-THEFT SYSTEM CONSISTS OF LEAVING YOUR VEHICLE UNPLUGGED.

APRIL SHOWERS BRING... MUD BOGGING!

IT'S OFFICIALLY SPRING WHEN YOU START FINDING ALL THE PUCKS THAT YOU LOST OVER THE WINTER.

YOU DON'T GO TO THE GYM TO WORK ON YOUR CALVES.

RING!

YOU'VE NEVER FOUND A NEEDLE IN A HAYSTACK, HOWEVER YOU **HAVE** FOUND YOUR SMARTPHONE IN STRAW BEDDING.

YOU MAKE SURE YOUR MOUTH IS CLOSED WHILE ADMIRING CANADA GEESE FLYING OVERHEAD.

IT STARTS SNOWING WHILE YOU'RE GETTING YOUR
WINTER TIRES TAKEN OFF.

ONE OF THE IRONS IN YOUR BAG IS A BRANDING IRON

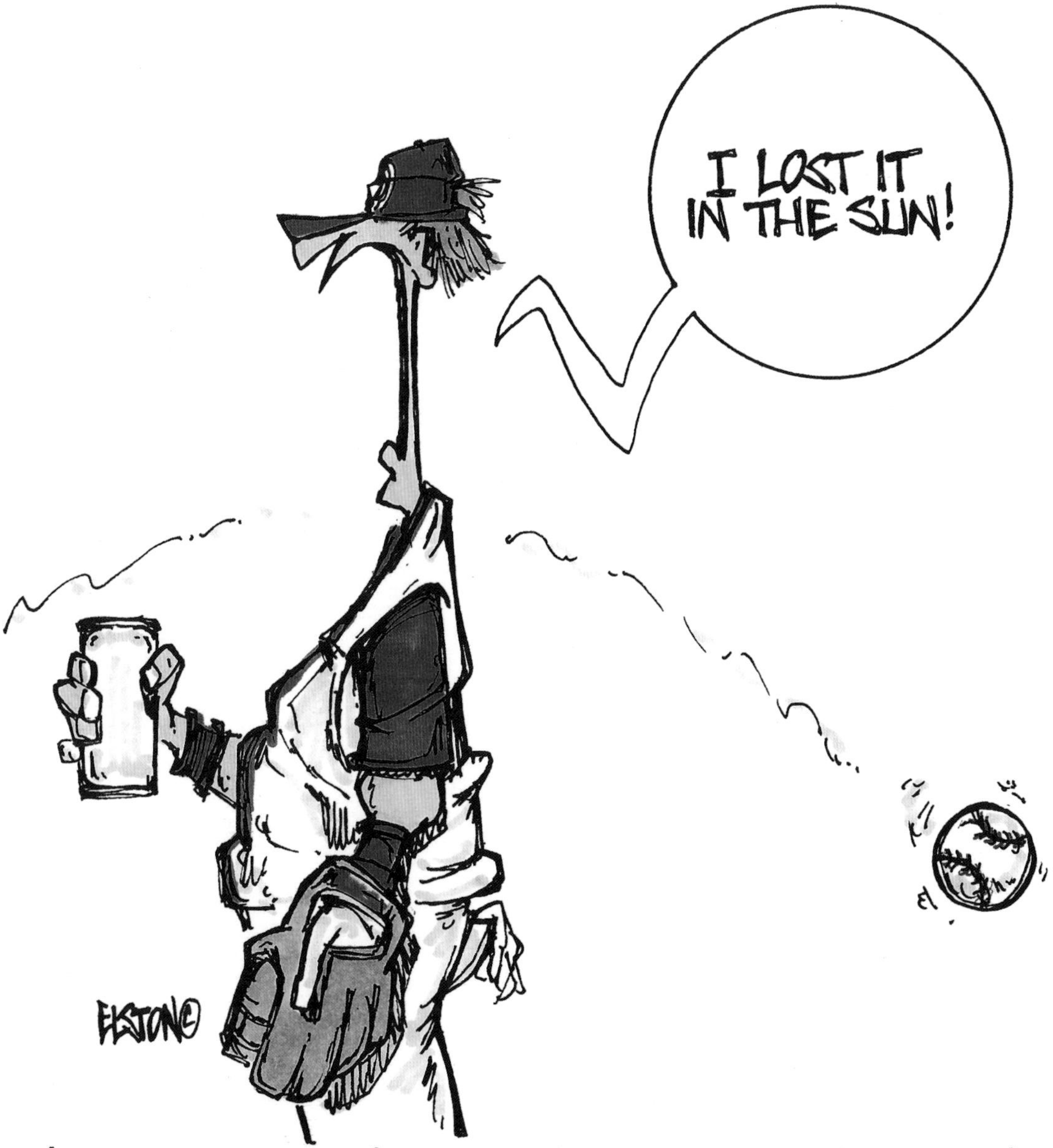
I LOST IT IN THE SUN!
ELSTON©

IT'S 10:30 PM IN YOUR JUNE 21ST SLO-PITCH GAME AND YOU CAN STILL CLAIM...

YOU WONDER IF THERE'S ANY FISH IN THIS "LAKE-OF-FIRE" EVERYBODY KEEPS TALKING ABOUT.

YOU'VE PLANTED YOUR GARDEN BEFORE THE MAY LONG WEEKEND...
AND REPLANTED IT AFTER.

WHEN DRIVING YOUR CAR, ALL CYCLISTS ARE IDIOTS
BUT WHEN YOU'RE CYCLING, ALL CAR DRIVERS ARE.

YOU DON'T CALL DRINKING AT 10:00 AM A PROBLEM—
YOU CALL IT CAMPING.

YOU CAN NAME CALGARY'S THREE WESTERNMOST SUBURBS.

YOUR IDEA OF "ROUGHING IT" IS SWITCHING FROM THE FIREPLACE CHANNEL TO THE CAMPFIRE CHANNEL

WHEN PEOPLE ASK WHAT YOU FARM
YOU TELL THEM, "GOPHERS AND DANDELIONS."

ROYALTY IS TOLD "IF YOUR HAT FALLS OFF YOUR HEAD BETTER BE IN IT."

YOU MAKE $35.00 AN HOUR BUT WILL WAIT IN A THREE HOUR LINE-UP FOR FREE PANCAKES.

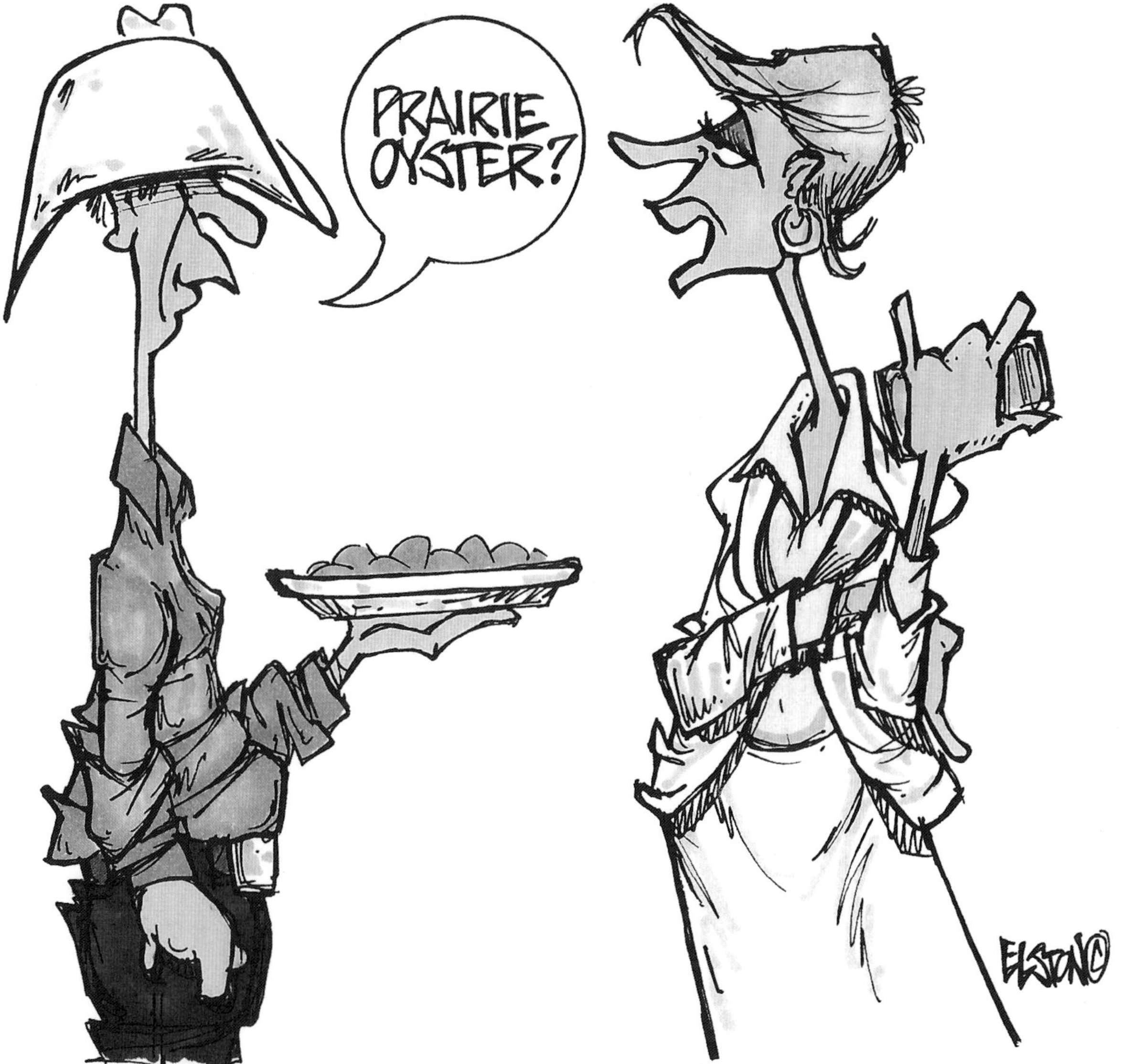
PRAIRIE OYSTER?
ELSTON©

YOU FIND IT HARD TO KEEP A STRAIGHT FACE WHILE OFFERING A TORONTONIAN A...

YOU KNOW THEY'RE PRONOUNCED "SHAPS".

AFTER A NIGHT OF STAMPEDING, YOU SET OFF THE SOUR GAS ALARM AT WORK

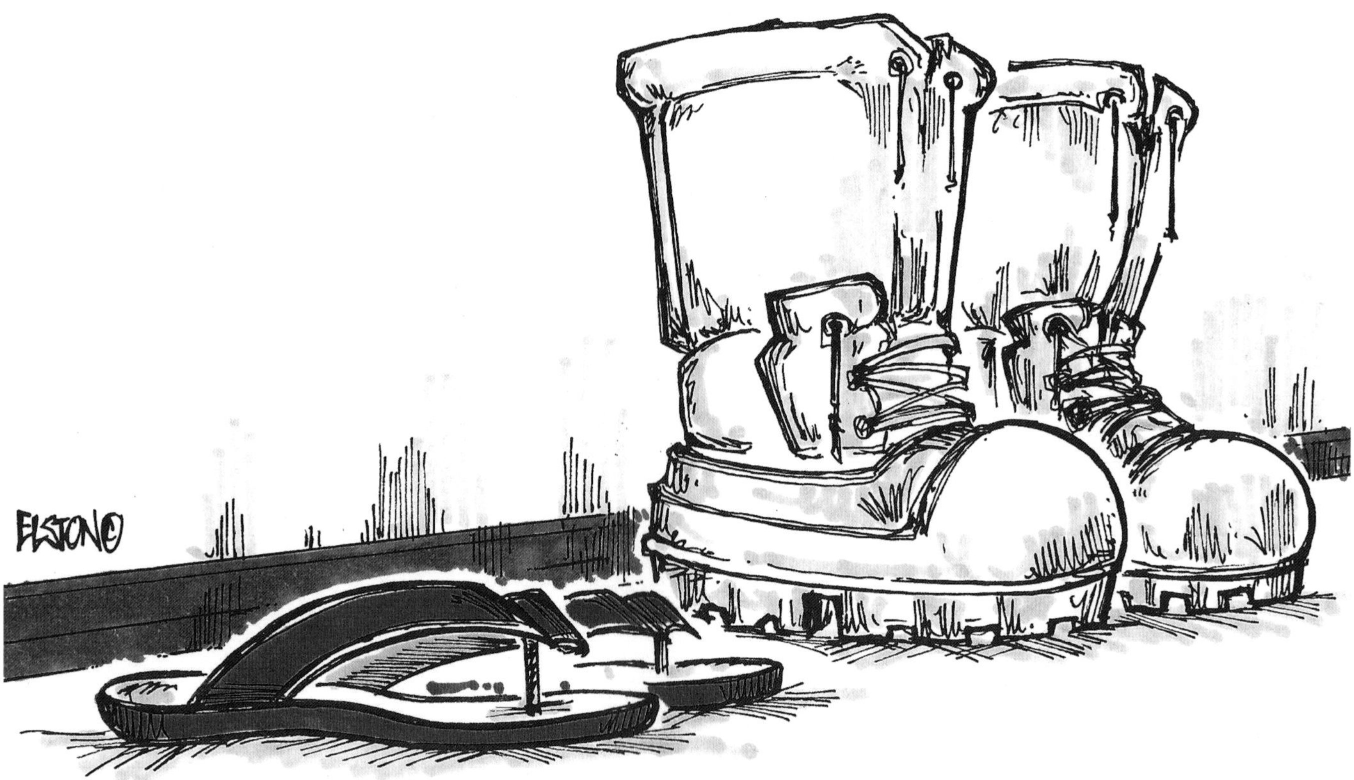
ELSTON©

THIS IS YOUR BACK PORCH.